One-Minute Prayers™

to End Your Day

Text by Hope Lyda

ONE-MINUTE PRAYERS™ TO END YOUR DAY
Copyright © 2007 by Harvest House Publishers
Published by Harvest House Publishers
Eugene, Oregon 97402

ISBN-13: 978-0-7369-1969-2
ISBN-10: 0-7369-1969-4

Printed in the United States of America

07 08 09 10 11 12 13 14 / BP-SK / 10 9 8 7 6 5 4 3 2 1

Contents

High Above

He also made the stars. God set them in the expanse of the sky to give light on the earth, to govern the day and the night, and to separate light from darkness. And God saw that it was good.

GENESIS 1:16-18

∽

Stars twinkle beyond my reach, but not above my faith. Nothing exceeds the extent of my hope in You. When I consider the people of the world, there are too many to count. Am I not just one of Your many children? How do You have time to hear my prayers, my concerns, my celebrations?

Then I consider how You made the stars. You placed them with care in the sky. There are so many—too many to count. Yet Your care is evident when those night beacons shine brightly and lead me back to belief in a God who knows me intimately, personally, and who hears each prayer that leaves my lips.

Transformation

First Time

*And God said, "Let there be light," and there was
light. God saw that the light was good, and he sep-
arated the light from the darkness. God called the
light "day," and the darkness he called "night." And
there was evening, and there was morning—the
first day.*

GENESIS 1:3-5

❧

I wonder what the first night looked like. How did
You arrange the sky? Did You watch the sun go down
and imagine how Your future creation would love the
sight of such beauty?

Lord, I thank You for that time when day becomes
night. I allow that time to come and go so very often
without speaking words of gratitude. Tonight I paid
attention to how You transformed the view from my
window. It reminded me of the hope I have in how You
are transforming me.

Goodness of a Bad Day

*Though outwardly we are wasting away, yet inwardly
we are being renewed day by day. For our light and
momentary troubles are achieving for us an eternal
glory that far outweighs them all.*

2 CORINTHIANS 4:16-17

೧

Today was a series of errors, miscommunications,
and missteps. It'd be nice to forget about the day, but I
know that while I am experiencing those bumps in the
road there are more eternal activities in play.

When I stumble, there is still victory. You transform
my very human errors into pearls of internal value. I
have learned humility, perseverance, faith, and patience.
Not bad for a day's work.

New Thoughts

Do not conform any longer to the pattern of this world, but be transformed by the renewing of your mind.

ROMANS 12:2

❧

I like stability. I like it so much that I unintentionally create each day to look the same as the last. I fall into ruts that do nothing to serve You or this life You have given to me. I pray for the wisdom to infuse my life with renewal and possibility.

When I am burdened with repetition and routine, remind me how much each day is worth. Change my thinking when I maneuver on autopilot. I don't want to waste the chance to think differently, feel differently, and to taste the different moments that add up to my lifetime.

Flip of a Switch

*I will turn the darkness into light before them and
make the rough places smooth.*

ISAIAH 42:16

∽

Just like that, day is night. And when I am sleeping,
the switch is flipped the other direction and night
becomes day. God, You orchestrate the universe without
need of my help. Your power does not depend on me.
I am so humbled that You work through me, and that
You see value in who I am and in this life I am living.

I find peace tonight, resting in the knowledge that
You orchestrated my existence. You turn my personal
night—the rough places I stumble over—into smooth
paths that reflect Your light. I am in good hands...they
are shaping me into a better person, just like that.

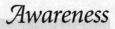

Awareness

Ritual

*Every morning and evening they present burnt
offerings and fragrant incense to the LORD.*

2 CHRONICLES 13:11

❧

I gave You my day today, Lord. With great intention, I handed over my emotions, my worries, my work, my relationships, and my steps. I feel the difference as the day comes to a close. I am more aware of how You are a part of all that I am, do, say, and feel. Oh, how many days I have wasted by not being aware of this truth!

Help me give my day to You again tomorrow. May I start and end all my days by presenting to You the offering of my life, of myself. And may this sacrifice be pleasing to You.

Forecast

[Jesus] replied, "When evening comes, you say, 'It will be fair weather, for the sky is red,' and in the morning, 'Today it will be stormy, for the sky is red and overcast.' You know how to interpret the appearance of the sky, but you cannot interpret the signs of the times."

MATTHEW 16:2-3

❧

I love to check the weather forecasts for the week. When I gather all the facts I feel more in control. I receive a sense of security. Getting the temperatures, examining the details, and knowing how the clouds will cover the sky might help me plan a family picnic, but that does not give me Your full knowledge or Your power.

I don't have to know what the weather is for tomorrow. Life is not built on predictions. It is built on Your truth, rain or shine.

Loose Change

*Command them to do good, to be rich in good
deeds, and to be generous and willing to share. In
this way they will lay up treasure for themselves
as a firm foundation for the coming age, so that
they may take hold of the life that is truly life.*

1 TIMOTHY 6:18-19

∽

When I come home, I reach into my pockets and
remove any coins remaining from a day of spending. A
jar on the counter holds these leftover portions that I
once considered hardly worth saving. As the jar grows
heavy, I understand the power of accumulation.

Lord, help me be aware of ways to spend goodness
throughout the day. May I never consider a portion of
kindness too small or insignificant to receive or give.
I know that each act of compassion accumulates in
heaven.

Counting Before Sleep

How precious to me are your thoughts, O God!
How vast is the sum of them! Were I to count
them, they would outnumber the grains of sand.
When I awake, I am still with you.

PSALM 139:17-18

∽

After a day of multitasking and problem solving, I have a hard time unwinding. My thoughts can rev up, spiral down, or pull me toward energy when I would rather be resting. I turn to You and seek Your thoughts, God. Fill my mind and my heart with Your peaceful, living words. When I call out to You, You are there.

Ending my day with You, Lord, gives me the security I have always longed for. I know that when I am awake, You will be with me. And when I am asleep, You are with me then too.

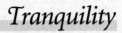

Tranquility

As the Storm Passes

*[Jesus] got up and rebuked the wind and the
raging waters; the storm subsided, and all was
calm. "Where is your faith?" he asked his disciples.*

LUKE 8:24-25

∾

When the air stirs about me, when the wind blows
from all directions, when I cannot stand because of the
pressure around me…I want to be a person of faith.
My eyes peer toward the dark night, and I cannot dis-
tinguish shapes. There is so much left unknown. Yet
my heart does not race and my mind does not doubt
because I know where my faith is—it is in the hope
of the moment, it is in the belief that the storm will
pass, it is in the assurance that Your peace overcomes
everything I will face.

Who I Am

Finally, all of you, live in harmony with one another; be sympathetic, love as brothers, be compassionate and humble.

1 PETER 3:8

∽

My mind mellows now, and I sit back, glad to be done with a busy day. Evening's tranquility presents a chance to settle in with myself and with You. It is the time of day that I most often reflect on who I am and what my life means.

I am filled with the desire to be more like You in every way. I want to feel compassion for others. I want to love my neighbor as myself. I want sympathy to turn my heart toward empathy. I want to follow Your ways and always know who I am—Your child.

My Haven

*He stilled the storm to a whisper; the waves of the
sea were hushed. They were glad when it grew
calm, and he guided them to their desired haven.*

PSALM 107:29-30

∽

I am glad to put my feet up. My bones were weary
today. I felt frazzled when I had to juggle two things
at once. My mouth barely functioned when I had to
speak. Oh, how I longed for this moment to breathe
deeply without the pressure to perform or please.

Lord, the whirlwind of worldly demands some-
times consumes me. Turn my thoughts to You and my
heart toward the peace You offer. When I do, I know
You will lead me to the haven of Your shelter.

What I Hold Tonight

They will speak of the glorious splendor of your majesty, and I will meditate on your wonderful works.

PSALM 145:5

∽

How lucky I am to see evidence of Your love and beauty. It surrounds me. Every moment offers a glimpse of Your caring touch if I open my eyes to it. Nature attests to Your splendor. A community gathering together during a time of need shines with Your brilliance. A child's unfiltered joy reflects Your own.

Lord, I cradle these images of You in my soul tonight. I meditate on Your wonderful works because they speak of Your goodness and faithfulness.

Darkness

When Darkness Follows

But let him remember the days of darkness, for they will be many.

ECCLESIASTES 11:8

✑

As night falls, it feels very familiar. My heart knows it well even during the daylight hours. A heaviness, the blanket of worry, covers me lately. Lord, bring me out of this constant night. Allow me to remember the days of darkness from before because when I think of them, I also am reminded of Your saving grace.

Walk with me through this time of shadows. Keep the darkness from following me into tomorrow. Protect me with the covering of hope.

Not Me, Lord

*When evening came, Jesus was reclining at the
table with the Twelve. And while they were eating,
he said, "I tell you the truth, one of you will betray
me." They were very sad and began to say to him
one after the other, "Surely not I, Lord?"*

MATTHEW 26:20-22

❧

Under the cloak of darkness, it is easy to lie. It
is easy to even tell myself half-truths when I am certain that I can stay protected by the veil of shadows.
Thoughts that would seem impossible during the cheer
of day, now flood my mind and weigh me down.

Lord, turn my negativity into an opportunity for
healing. In the past I have said, "Surely not I, Lord…"
But now I know how vulnerable I am. I will tell myself
and You the truth: I cannot overcome my self-decep-
tion with self-talk. I need You and Your light to be
present.

My Worth

For I am poor and needy, and my heart is wounded within me. I fade away like an evening shadow; I am shaken off like a locust.

PSALM 109:22-23

∽

I have been comparing myself to others again. Yes, this is a road I have taken many times. Why can't I learn to place my value solely in You rather than in the fickle preferences of the world? I don't earn enough, have enough, know enough…I am not enough when I stand alone.

Only You can shine light upon my beauty. My goodness exists because I have placed my faith in who You are. I will never be perfect by comparison to an ever-changing list of worldly requirements. But I will always be wealthy, I will have abundance, and I will be enough when I rest in Your purpose for my life.

The Light Show

*You are my lamp, O Lord; the Lord turns my
darkness into light.*

2 SAMUEL 22:29

❧

A friend reminded me of how far I had come.
They knew me back when I had sorrow and empti-
ness. Now they notice the light that burns from within.
They remember me when I was eager to turn a good
moment into a gripe session and when I felt encouraged by another's discouragement.

You have turned the direction of my heart, my feet,
my mind, and my actions. Since I have known You,
the frown of yesterday rarely crosses my countenance.
Even when trials are on the horizon, I know to follow
the light of Your way. And You take me far.

Restless

Resting in Promises

Moses also said, "You will know that it was the
LORD when he gives you meat to eat in the eve-
ning and all the bread you want in the morning,
because he has heard your grumbling against him."

EXODUS 16:8

∽

Why don't I learn to be quiet? I have been grumbling about my circumstances for so long that even I
cannot bear to listen. When others face bigger troubles,
I am quick to suggest my turmoil is of great weight and
concern. I tell my story of woe over and over.

Lord, You silence my restless spirit and my ram-
pant complaints. I look around me at the provision so
obviously from Your hand, and I am unable to find the
silly words that flowed easily before. Peace overcomes
me, and I rest in the promises that shine forth even
when I do not deserve them.

Which Way to Go?

*Sow your seed in the morning, and at evening let
not your hands be idle, for you do not know which
will succeed, whether this or that, or whether both
will do equally well.*

ECCLESIASTES 11:6

∽

Should I go this way...or that way? Tomorrow I will
face a fork in the road, and both directions will look so
very tempting. This question keeps me awake because
I have allowed myself to become restless. Pacing in the
living room does not still my mind or my heart. Give
me an answer, Lord. Please.

You remind me to fall to my knees in prayer and
supplication and thanksgiving. My hands reach for Your
Word, and this purpose calms them. Now I am feeding
my spirit with certainty over uncertainty. And this night
I give my doubts over to Your control.

Chasing Fears

*So do not worry, saying, "What shall we eat?" or
"What shall we drink?" or "What shall we wear?"
For the pagans run after all these things, and your
heavenly Father knows that you need them. But
seek first his kingdom and his righteousness, and
all these things will be given to you as well.*

MATTHEW 6:31-33

∽

It is futile to chase after fear, for fear leaves in
its wake a very new path of problems. The people I
want to guarantee me security are only people. Their
promises do not mean anything to me and my eternal
future.

I will not waste my time, my day, my evening in
this pursuit of unnecessary concerns. I need not glance
around nervously, anticipating the next problem. You
assure me that I need only to look to You and Your
kingdom. Here true needs are recognized, and they are
filled, satisfied by Your grace.

This, I'm Not Good At

Be still before the LORD and wait patiently for him.

PSALM 37:7

ℴ

I have loved You for so long, Lord. I have become a person who prays earnestly and with vulnerability. My speech is becoming filled with words of encouragement and hope. I seek Your Word with deep hunger because there were too many years when I sought nourishment from empty sources.

But God...I am not good at being still before You. There is a part of me that wants to rush the process, wants to leap forward to the promise fulfilled, and wants to take the reins of my life from Your hands. Help me grow in patience. Keep me from the desire to disrupt Your plan for my life. I am ready for this lesson.

Refuge

What I Call Sacred

One man considers one day more sacred than
another; another man considers every day alike.
Each one should be fully convinced in his own mind.

ROMANS 14:5

༄

This time of the evening feels sacred. I believe it is the point in my day when I am able to give myself over to Your presence. I want to take this sense of peace with me into my chaotic days. What a gift that would be.

For now I will rest in what I know to be true. You are here with me. This time of refuge and connection provides me with a view of Your faithfulness, compassion, and desire to be present with Your child.

Shelter Me

Keep me safe, O God, for in you I take refuge.

PSALM 16:1

∽

Shelter me tonight, Lord. Take me in Your embrace and keep me safe from my past and my future worries. If left on my own, I would not make it through the night without a stream of tears. But here in Your arms I can relax. I think more clearly from this place of refuge.

I used to be a child who didn't know to come in out of the rain. Now I am Your child who knows to come in to Your presence and out of the pain. Don't let go of me, Lord.

Mine and Yours

*In your unfailing love you will lead
the people you have redeemed.
In your strength you will guide them
to your holy dwelling.*

EXODUS 15:13

∽

This is quite a journey I am on. Each day offers more steps toward Your holy dwelling, Your resting place. When I stumble, You whisper to me that I am worth leading. You reach for my hand and help me to stand and continue.

My weakness is Your strength. My failing is Your victory. My worst-case scenario is Your moment of shining glory. Lord, You shape all my humanness with Your power and grace, and it becomes something new. This is the miraculous journey of redemption.

Refuge Within

Create in me a pure heart, O God, and renew a
steadfast spirit within me.

PSALM 51:10

❧

I have sought to create a sense of refuge in many different ways. I got organized—and that lasted a couple weeks. I tried some breathing practices to relieve stress but was afraid I was doing them wrong. I sprinkled potpourri in my bedroom, but started sneezing.

God, now I understand that my true chance for refuge will not happen by altering the external factors. May Your purity stir within me and create a sanctuary where Your love will make its home.

Solitude

Home with the Lord

We live by faith, not by sight. We are confident, I say, and would prefer to be away from the body and at home with the Lord.

2 CORINTHIANS 5:7-8

❧

As soon as I step away from the conversations with others, the distractions, and the busyness, my heart's first impulse is to run to You. When I am alone and experiencing solitude, I am also experiencing Your presence with more intensity.

During times of aloneness, my faith in You seems clearer, brighter, and stronger. It is because I am leaning on You completely. There is no greater peace than to be at home with You. I have faith that this is a mere echo of what it feels like to go home to heaven.

Head for the Hills

After he had dismissed them, [Jesus] went up on a
mountainside by himself to pray.
When evening came, he was there alone.

MATTHEW 14:23

❦

I am following Your lead, Lord. I get it now more than ever. Your most difficult times were covered and followed with prayer. After long days of praying over others and healing them, You still yearned to pray to Your Father.

There is so much going on in my life. Good things. Hard things. Some things that I have yet to figure out. I am learning to bring all to You in prayer and to seek Your face no matter the circumstances. It is time to unwind, but my heart is heading for the hills to spend moments of solitude with its Maker.

Hear My Cries

Evening, morning and noon I cry out in distress,
and he hears my voice.

PSALM 55:17

∽

I am like an infant who needs comfort, food, and reassurance around the clock. I cry out to You in the morning when I am pondering what questions the day might present. I seek to connect with You when the day is going full speed and I need a right perspective to survive. In the evening, my cries are even greater. It is the hour of solitude; I need to know that You are with me even as distractions fall away and I am left vulnerable and silent. Hear my cries, Abba Father.

Only You

My soul finds rest in God alone; my salvation
comes from him.

PSALM 62:1

∽

Lord, when You look at my past, does it hurt You to see the many times I tried to save myself? Or when I asked others to save me? I avoided being alone with You because I wasn't ready to exchange my version of salvation for Yours. I didn't believe I was worth the grace.

Solitude no longer scares me. I welcome it because my soul rests in Your hands. I don't want to find this comfort anywhere else. Only You can save me. Only now can I see that Your love makes me worthy.

Covering

Completely Covered

But just as you excel in everything—in faith, in speech, in knowledge, in complete earnestness and in your love for us—see that you also excel in this grace of giving.

2 CORINTHIANS 8:7

∽

Did I honor You today, Lord? All day I was striving to be godly when I spoke, made choices, did work, expressed kindness, prayed—I think that covers it. Are You proud of me for making a conscious effort to walk in Your ways?

Now when I am here with You, recapping the day and trying to get a report card summary out of You, I realize how ineffective and faithless this thinking is. You have not called me to be perfect; You have called me to be covered by Your perfect grace.

Gladness

*Let all who take refuge in you be glad; let them
ever sing for joy. Spread your protection over
them, that those who love your name may rejoice
in you.*

PSALM 5:11

∽

I have many blessings, yet my spirit leans toward
sorrow or frustration so naturally. Guide me to the
refuge of Your mercy, Lord. When I know I am covered
by You and cared for by You, I embrace gladness.

My spirits are lifted when I am in fellowship
with You. Calling out Your name and relying on Your
name brings me deep joy. May I always trust in
Your love and comfort, and may I always step under
Your protection.

Special Delivery

You are my hiding place; you will protect me from trouble and surround me with songs of deliverance.

PSALM 32:7

∽

I have my dry cleaning delivered to my home. I can order pizza to arrive at my door within 20 minutes. But there is nothing I can do to deliver myself from the trouble that plagues me tonight. I have tried. I have prayed for You to give me the strength to do it on my own, when all along I needed the protection of Your strength.

It's not easy for me to ask for comfort and help. I am stubborn and human and often conflicted with a false sense of control. Pare away these excuses, Lord. I am in great need, and only You can deliver me.

Banner of Love

See how I love your precepts; preserve my life, O
LORD, according to your love.

PSALM 119:159

✎

I remember singing a song as a child at camp
about the banner of Your love. I never understood that
song. But now that evening doesn't end with festivities
involving marshmallows and bonfires, the meaning of
those words is becoming as clear as a summer night's
sky.

Beneath the banner of Your love and Your wisdom,
my life is preserved. My adult problems outweigh those
I took with me to camp, but even so, they are not too
great for Your healing and Your grace to cover. This is
something to sing about!

Reflection

What Comes to Mind

*You kept my eyes from closing; I was too troubled
to speak. I thought about the former days, the years
of long ago; I remembered my songs in the night.*

PSALM 77:4-6

৵

I have been staring at the ceiling for hours. I feel
the urgency to talk to You tonight. But there is silence,
so I stare and wonder and ponder. Then I begin to
remember all the times You have been there for me. All
the times I watched with amazement as You shaped a
trial into a treasure.

You speak to me tonight through these remem-
brances. I am not alone. I never have been. And this
is what You remind me of over and over through Your
acts of faithfulness.

Tell Me

*But make up your mind not to worry beforehand
how you will defend yourselves. For I will give you
words and wisdom that none of your adversaries
will be able to resist or contradict.*

LUKE 21:14-15

૭

Just when I think I have everything all figured out,
somebody challenges me or tears down my securities.
The right words never seem to rise to my mind and to
my mouth to dispute what they are saying, so here I
am wanting to figure it all out beforehand. I don't want
any surprises tomorrow. Help me, Lord.

Peace comes over me as I ask for Your help. You
are not going to provide me with advance comments
to memorize before confrontation. Instead, You tell me
to reflect on Your faithfulness and goodness, and the
words and strength I need will be there.

Life Management

*The hardworking farmer should be the first to receive
a share of the crops. Reflect on what I am saying, for
the Lord will give you insight into all this.*

2 TIMOTHY 2:6-7

∽

I have an entire shelf of life-management books.
They offer some wisdom and some advice, but they
fall short of insight that relates to my life specifically.
How grateful I am that I have Your truth and Your
Word to reflect on.

You don't generalize or tell me the top five ways I
will improve my existence or my bank account. You
tell me there is just one way to manage my life—to
give it over to You. My hard work will possibly reap
character development, financial support, and positive
results. But I never have to earn Your grace—this is the
key to success.

Everything in Its Place

When I consider your heavens, the work of your fingers, the moon and the stars, which you have set in place, what is man that you are mindful of him, the son of man that you care for him?

PSALM 8:3-4

ﾎ

Tonight's sky tells me much of Your nature. When I reflect on the miracle of starlight, the pull of the moon, the orbit of the earth, and the mysteries of space, I feel small and insignificant. But then I consider how much order and brilliance it took to construct this night sky, and I know what I need to know to have hope: The same care and attention went into the creation of me.

When You placed my heart just so and aligned my purpose with Your will, there was nothing left to chance. I don't need to question whether You think of me because Your fingers shaped me. This life You have set in motion is here for a reason.

Dusk

Looking for Light

He has blocked my way so I cannot pass; he has shrouded my paths in darkness.

JOB 19:8

∽

Dusk covers the road ahead. Different colors are cast against the sky as though a new artist were on shift. I squint, trying to see what usually is clear on the horizon.

I know it is time to get home because soon there will be no light to ease my journey. My soul craves more light. You have shrouded my path in darkness. I cannot continue with my own vision, but must trust Your sight to lead me through to tomorrow's dawn.

First, Praise

Give glory to the LORD your God before he brings the darkness, before your feet stumble on the darkening hills.

JEREMIAH 13:16

൜

Thank You for today, Lord! I praise Your name and give You the glory for all that was accomplished. May You look at what this servant has done and call it good and right. Today was not easy, but I kept hold of Your Word and my path was secured.

I know the darkness will come. There will be a time when I have trials that pull me from the path and cast me onto the rocky terrain of uncertainty and risk. On this slope I will hold on to my faith—a faith that has been strengthened through my days of praise.

Sins of Shadows

The eye of the adulterer watches for dusk; he thinks, "No eye will see me," and he keeps his face concealed.

JOB 24:15

✽

There are those who seek anonymity as shadows create hiding places ideal for concealing sins—from human eyes. May I never allow the appearance of clouds during times of trial to become my excuse to betray You, Lord.

In faith, there is never an absence of light. Total darkness will not conceal my wrongdoings. Reveal to me any part of my life that has been left to the shadows. Give me the courage to bring indiscretions to You with a spirit of repentance and sorrow so that I never boast with pride that I have kept something from You.

Bright with Belief

But when he asks, he must believe and not doubt,
because he who doubts is like a wave of the sea,
blown and tossed by the wind.

JAMES 1:6

∽

Illuminate the answers, Lord. Convict my spirit and turn me in the direction of clarity and truth. I have doubted in the past, and it made for a very bumpy voyage. When I stare out at the horizon, I want to believe there is a way through the storm. Doubt is a clouding of the mind and heart, and it disturbs any chance I have to navigate with faith.

When I ask for direction and Your beacon shines to guide me, may I never look back to the dark waves behind me. Anchor my belief in the sureness of the shore that is Your purpose and hope.

Worry

Worst Case Scenario

*In the morning you will say, "If only it were evening!"
and in the evening, "If only it were morning!"*

DEUTERONOMY 28:67

❧

The flip-flop of worry turns my thoughts, my
stomach, and my hope upside down. Instead of
standing firm in Your promises, I waver back and forth,
uncertain of what I want or need. All day I longed for
the quiet and solitary nature of night. Now, in the later
hours, I can pray fervently to make it until the light
of dawn.

Lord, speak to my soul. Grant me the wisdom and
faith to see that there is no place or time or situation
that will distance me from Your sight or Your peace.

Missing Out

*As evening approached, the disciples came to him
and said, "This is a remote place, and it's already
getting late. Send the crowds away, so they can go
to the villages and buy themselves some food."*

MATTHEW 14:15

∾

I planned and replanned my day today. Yet there
were surprises at every turn. Some were blessings,
some I hope were blessings in disguise...but they all
disrupted my big plans. I like to be efficient, Lord.
When things closed in on me, I became anxious about
the outcome.

But just as You showed the disciples time after time,
there is no need to worry. Things are in Your control.
When I worry, I lose sight of the purpose in that very
moment. Help me see Your hand in everything that
happens—including the detours.

Choke Hold

The one who received the seed that fell among the thorns is the man who hears the word, but the worries of this life and the deceitfulness of wealth choke it, making it unfruitful.

MATTHEW 13:22

∾

I want a faith that flourishes, Lord. I want to hear Your promises and take hold of them and believe in them. But when my worries about money, relationships, or the day's agenda kick in, my faith suffers. My fears stunt its growth, and I am left feeling empty.

Let me be encouraged by other believers and uplifted by creation's wonder. Hope creates a fertile ground where faith can take root and blossom. Guide me toward those people and practices that will inspire me to live a fruitful, abundant life.

Out and In

[The Lord] will never let the righteous fall.

PSALM 55:22

∽

I hung up the phone after talking to a friend about a problem. I sat in my favorite chair with my favorite blanket and dissected the problem further. I made a list of possible solutions but nothing seemed remarkable enough to work, so I kept on worrying. Finally I sought Your Word, Lord, and was reminded to cast my cares on You.

I wanted someone to take my problem away. But Your promise is to walk with me, to sustain me, to hold me up as I make my way through this in Your strength. You pull me out of the despair and promise to never let me fall.

Lessons

Before the Rain

*Do the skies themselves send down showers? No, it
is you, O LORD our God. Therefore our hope is in
you, for you are the one who does all this.*

JEREMIAH 14:22

❧

I opened my window tonight during a passing
storm. My lungs took in the fresh air, and I was so
thankful that the clouds had brought renewal to a
thirsty Earth. But before I heard the first drops on
my roof, You had commanded the showers. You are
behind everything beautiful and wondrous.

Tonight I benefit from Your sweet rain. I learn a
lesson about hope: It is to be placed in You, the maker
of the smallest and the largest blessings.

In Your Hands

I form the light and create darkness,
I bring prosperity and create disaster;
I, the LORD, do all these things.

ISAIAH 45:7

∽

It is so easy to take credit for accomplishments or milestones in my life. Yet it is You who formed the light and created darkness. This morning I found myself accepting praise for something that was entirely Your doing.

My heart lesson tonight is to give You glory for all that happens. You, Lord, do all that is good in my life and throughout my days. I cheat myself out of a deeper faith when I take credit for wonders shaped by my Creator.

Seed of Faith

*I would like to learn just one thing from you: Did
you receive the Spirit by observing the law, or by
believing what you heard?*

GALATIANS 3:2

∽

Does my faith reveal a strong sense of Your saving
grace and Your love? I ask tonight because lately my
motives seem so much about bringing justice to situations and relationships. I first came to You because
of Your compassion and Your forgiveness, so why do
I seem determined to pass judgment rather than to
give mercy?

Help me learn to treat others with the love You
have shown me. Maybe I will plant the seed of faith
in another's heart.

Always My Teacher

When [Jesus] had finished washing their feet, he put on his clothes and returned to his place. "Do you understand what I have done for you?" he asked them. "You call me 'Teacher' and 'Lord,' and rightly so, for that is what I am. Now that I, your Lord and Teacher, have washed your feet, you also should wash one another's feet. I have set you an example that you should do as I have done for you.

JOHN 13:12-15

∽

The role models of faith around me are people who keep learning from You. Give me a hunger for the lessons You have to teach me. I want to follow Your example with passion and purpose. When You washed the feet of Your disciples, You did not call them to praise You, but to turn around and wash the feet of others. This is Your powerful lesson to Your children. May I become a forever student of the Master.

Peace

Daily Sweetness

Light is sweet, and it pleases the eyes to see the sun. However many years a man may live, let him enjoy them all.

ECCLESIASTES 11:7-8

❧

Thank You for this day. When I stepped outside and felt the warmth of the sun on my face, I was filled with gratitude. I don't always recognize my days as gifts. They can blur together into a string of indistinguishable moments. But I am learning to enjoy my life, bit by bit.

Lord, give me a desire for my own life. Help me exchange grumblings for peaceful prayers. May I always feel the warmth of Your light and celebrate each day fully.

What I Say I Want

I have no peace, no quietness;
I have no rest, but only turmoil.

JOB 3:26

∽

"If only I could have some peace and quiet," I said to a friend the other day. Yet in the evening when I have a chance for serenity, I create distractions. God, why do I set myself up for chaos? Maybe I'm afraid of spending time alone with my thoughts and feelings.

I want to rest in You and lean into the quiet. Still my thoughts and show me how to make quality time for myself and for You. And the next time I wish for the wonder of silence, I will actually know what I am talking about.

When the World Sleeps

Those living far away fear your wonders;
where morning dawns and evening fades
you call forth songs of joy.

PSALM 65:8

❧

Others are sleeping, and the night is filled with sounds of nocturnal life. Normally I would be frustrated about the lack of sleep, but tonight I like the tranquility. I like talking to You, knowing that You don't slumber but are with me every moment.

I can call out to You in the cave of night or the sky of day. Your omnipresence assures me at any hour. Before the dawn, the lullaby of Your voice is clear, and my spirit joins in.

Giving Over

Submit to God and be at peace with him; in this way prosperity will come to you. Accept instruction from his mouth and lay up his words in your heart.

JOB 22:21-22

I listen for Your instruction, Lord. I want to give myself over to Your leading and Your will. Provide me with a discerning heart so I do not listen to my own wants but am attentive and open to Your desires for my life.

Each word that comes from You is a gift to treasure, to store up, to use, and to follow. Break down the walls I have built out of expectations and selfish demands. I am ready to receive the peace of Your life-giving wisdom.

Love

If Not Love

If I have the gift of prophecy and can fathom all mysteries and all knowledge, and if I have a faith that can move mountains, but have not love, I am nothing.

1 CORINTHIANS 13:2

When my days are difficult or I face trials where my own strength is useless, I know that I am held up by You. It is not only my faith that ties me to You, but it is Your love for me that gives me courage, hope, and the perseverance required.

I draw encouragement from understanding my gifts and my purpose in You, yet I know that these do not shape me, make me, or sustain me. Only Your love does that.

Empathy

*For I wrote you out of great distress and anguish
of heart and with many tears, not to grieve you
but to let you know the depth of my love for you.*

2 CORINTHIANS 2:4

❧

Lord, grant me a portion of Your heart for others. I do not always know what needs a person has or what sorrows he or she holds inside. Give me Your eyes to notice such things. It is easy to distance myself from the hurt of a stranger or even the struggles of friends who do not speak out. Give me a love so deep that it forgives, it covers, it embraces, and it protects the people You bring into my life.

Insight

*And this is my prayer: that your love may abound
more and more in knowledge and depth of insight, so
that you may be able to discern what is best and may
be pure and blameless until the day of Christ.*

PHILIPPIANS 1:9-10

✑

I have a friend who has great instinct for what to do
or what to say at any given moment. Meanwhile, I take
a step back, afraid that I might do the wrong thing and
make the situation worse. When does my faith lead to
a sense of confidence?

Infuse me with courage and insight, Lord. I know
it is my own insecurity that keeps me back in the
shadows and holds me in a pattern of indecision. This
also prevents me from demonstrating Your love and
Your power to others in my life. Tomorrow, I will step
out in faith in some way. It is time to live in Your
knowledge with confidence.

Love Is

May your unfailing love rest upon us, O LORD,
even as we put our hope in you.

PSALM 33:22

∽

Love is unfailing and uncompromising. Your love is a shining star in the night's sky that leads us forward and toward the hope of tomorrow. You know my steps before I ponder which way to go. You offer me free will so that I can choose to follow my Creator in love and submission.

I place my hope in You at all times. Help me to never invest myself and my faith in the things of the world.

Hope

Some Day

*But by faith we eagerly await through the Spirit
the righteousness for which we hope.*

GALATIANS 5:5

ॐ

Flashbacks from the day produce images of me making mistakes, missing opportunities, and sinning. I hardly noticed the little white lies or the insensitivities at the time. But I'm starting to become more aware of these indiscretions. My faith is moving me toward righteousness, but it will be Your grace that gets me there.

I'm starting to believe there is hope for me yet.

Counting on You

I will praise you forever for what you have done;
in your name I will hope, for your name is good.

PSALM 52:9

∽

When I speak of Your name and praise You for what
You have given to me and brought me through, some
people do not know how to respond. It makes them
uncomfortable because they have not experienced the
same. They have been let down by people; therefore,
it is hard for them to imagine a God who does not fail,
who does not leave.

I want to share hope in You. Grant me a gentle
spirit and give me an understanding heart so that I
might show Your goodness through my actions and
my continued praise.

Pray It, Don't Say It

*Do not let this Book of the Law depart from your
mouth; meditate on it day and night, so that you
may be careful to do everything written in it. Then
you will be prosperous and successful.*

JOSHUA 1:8

∽

My mouth has been eager to talk of Your mercy and
Your truth, but I am not good at meditating on Your
wisdom and Your law. I select bits of Your Word as I
need it to prove a point or to demonstrate my knowledge. How silly I can be. This is not serving You, and
it is not leading me to the purpose and prosperity You
long to give me.

Only when I own Your truths deep within my
mind, heart, and spirit can they produce fruit in my
life. Only when I commit to holding Your character
in esteem will I have the hope of becoming more like
You.

Faithfulness

A longing fulfilled is sweet to the soul.

PROVERBS 13:19

❧

God, You are so faithful to me. Your goodness surrounds me daily. I asked for help today, and You answered me in surprising ways. I felt vulnerable and needed a sense of protection and care—and You were there. I have longed for this kind of security all my life. Even with faith, I often doubted that You might be there to catch me should I fall.

But today I realized that the hunger is gone and fulfillment is in its place. You have met my longing with the sweetness of a future and a hope.

Nourishment

You Know Me

*You understand, O LORD; remember me and care
for me.*

JEREMIAH 15:15

∽

You see me when nobody else does. You know me
when nobody else inquires. You see me when others
look past me. You care for me when others are too
busy. Being Your child means I am nourished spiritu-
ally and emotionally even when I feel alone.

How many times have I looked to others to feed
me my sense of value? God, renew my strength and my
understanding of how much You care. I am known by
the Creator of the universe, and He loves me!

Strange Food

He humbled you, causing you to hunger and then feeding you with manna, which neither you nor your fathers had known, to teach you that man does not live on bread alone but on every word that comes from the mouth of the LORD.

DEUTERONOMY 8:3

∾

I have begged for assistance and for You to ease my hunger, Lord. There is so much that I want. My journey is difficult at times, and I seek support. I have asked over and over for You to send answers and understanding and help.

Lord, all this time You have been providing me with all that I need. My concerns are understood. My path might not look like I want it to, but You are paving it with Your promises if only I would pay attention. Your Word and these promises are different than the food I asked for, but they nourish me and renew my spirit.

Casting Cares

Cast your cares on the Lord and he will sustain you.

PSALM 55:22

⌇

What do people do when they don't have You in their lives? I lay awake tonight wondering where I would be if I hadn't met You. I am blessed with strong relationships and friendships, yet not one person in my life could handle the cares and worries I entrust to You.

Not only do You hear my troubles, but You exchange them for what I need in that moment and for the long journey. People provide pat answers; You provide eternal promises. I am grateful to bring my whole heart to You.

Source of Life

*You care for the land and water it; you enrich it
abundantly.*

PSALM 65:9

∽

Showers cleanse the air. Sun warms the soil. Winds
blow seeds across the land. Seasons set in motion by
Your hand nourish the plants and the people and the
generations of those who live beneath Your gaze.

My life feels like a complete system—a mini-
world—that depends on Your cleansing grace, the
warmth of Your compassion, and Your transforming
love. Help me harvest the seeds You have planted in
my soul. I know that abundance awaits me.

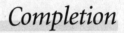

Completion

Here to There

Perseverance must finish its work so that you may
be mature and complete, not lacking anything.

JAMES 1:4

∽

As my day comes to a close, I think about the large gap between where I am and where I want to be. I don't mean financially or professionally, but in the ways of faith. I want to know You more intimately and take Your precepts to heart.

Each day is a new opportunity to become more Christlike. Hold me accountable, Lord. Keep me in the company of those who will encourage and challenge me. Between here to there is a leap of faith, but I'm ready for the strides required.

Looking for the Line

Now finish the work, so that your eager willing-
ness to do it may be matched by your completion
of it, according to your means.

2 CORINTHIANS 8:11

∾

My home is overrun with half-finished projects and
partially read books. I started and stopped four exer-
cise programs last year alone. So what makes me think
I can continue in my faith and complete the task of
growing in You? I don't know what the finish line will
look like, but I am watching for it. I am being perfected
in Your grace, and I am becoming more excited about
fulfilling Your purpose for my life.

The finish line is up ahead, and I know You are
shaping the twists and turns of my race to get me
there.

Reaching for the Baton

I have fought the good fight, I have finished the race, I have kept the faith.

2 TIMOTHY 4:7

∽

My pursuit of complete faith has become a relay. Lord, You have given me so many prayer warriors, encouragers, and godly examples to follow. Each one of them provides me with a baton of wisdom and the belief that I can go further. Now I eagerly watch for the next lesson that will mold my view of what it means to be Your child.

Past discouragements are completely out of view and out of mind. I have kept the faith, and You, Lord, have kept me fighting the good fight.

No More Settling

*However, I consider my life worth nothing to me,
if only I may finish the race and complete the task
the Lord Jesus has given me—the task of testifying
to the gospel of God's grace.*

ACTS 20:24

∽

All I wanted to accomplish today was to survive. My plate was so full, and I felt overwhelmed. How often do I settle for such a limited view of my day's purpose? "I just want to get by" turns into "Where did last month go?" I'm caught in a faithless rut.

Lord, give me a deeper vision for tomorrow. The completion of one day is the continuation of a bigger plan. I pray my life will be a testimony to Your grace. Turn my limited goals into grander, eternal passions.

Silence

Hold My Tongue

If you have anything to say, answer me; speak up,
for I want you to be cleared. But if not, then listen
to me; be silent, and I will teach you wisdom.

JOB 33:32-33

∽

God, I've never asked for this before, but I need to
learn to be silent. You have placed wise people in my
life who have advice and clear thinking to offer me. My
pride gets in the way, and I pretend to know what I
am doing. But I want to hear their truths. I want to be
open to what You are teaching me through them.

Hold my tongue, open my ears, and prepare my
heart for all You are saying to me.

Speaking with Actions

*For it is God's will that by doing good you should
silence the ignorant talk of foolish men.*

1 PETER 2:15

∽

As I think over the day, I realize there were many
opportunities to express my beliefs through my
actions. Lord, help me have a faith so real, so infused
throughout my being that I do not have to rely just on
words to express my love for You.

When I serve You by being compassionate, wise,
generous, forgiving, and loving, those who want to
undermine faith with false accusations or ignorant
comments will be silenced, and those who long to
know more about You will have a chance to "hear" the
good news.

Tears

O my God, I cry out by day, but you do not answer, by night, and am not silent.

PSALM 22:2

∽

Lord, do You hear my cries? I am lonely. Nighttime seems to echo with my sadness and even memories of past disappointments. The distractions of daytime seem so far away. I don't want to face this silence alone. I want to hear from You; I want to be certain You are right here beside me.

God listen to the brokenness of my spirit. I pray for comfort as I sit in the silence and accept the balm of Your presence.

Turning, Turning

*You turned my wailing into dancing; you removed
my sackcloth and clothed me with joy, that my
heart may sing to you and not be silent.*

PSALM 30:11-12

∽

My time of weeping has ended. The grieving that
once consumed me has dissipated into the night. My
heart is turning toward joy and life. My feet are turning
as I dance into a new stage.

Oh, how I have waited for You to turn my sorrow
to celebration. My lips cannot stop praising You and
singing of Your goodness. I want to tell the world that
You walk with us through the pain and You rejoice
with us in our day of healing. Hallelujah!

Listening

My Mother Taught Me

He who answers before listening—that is his folly and his shame.

PROVERBS 18:13

∽

During my childhood, I was sent to my room a few times for speaking out of turn. Usually I was trying to prove a point—a really good point, of course. Lord, I am not so different as an adult. I am eager to set the record straight. I don't even recognize this fault until it is too late and the words have been spoken.

Lord, convict me when my desire to clarify or correct is hindering a relationship, a conversation, a chance to listen with my whole heart.

What Catches My Attention

She had a sister called Mary, who sat at the Lord's feet listening to what he said. But Martha was distracted by all the preparations that had to be made.

LUKE 10:39-40

∽

I worry about my well-being, about my security and future. There is much to be done in order to provide for tomorrow. Such thoughts consume me. You are here with me, and still my mind races with to-do lists, figures, and concerns. Lord, steer me from the distractions that plague me. I want to be the one who will drop anything and everything—my plans, my expectations, my will—to spend time at Your feet.

Following You begins with listening to You. Let me put aside my agenda and sit at Your feet all my days.

Answer Buffet

But as for me, I watch in hope for the LORD, I wait
for God my Savior; my God will hear me.

MICAH 7:7

∼

The world has many answers. My concerns seem
ripe for the world's intervention. But I want my hope to
be in You alone. I am trying not to listen to advice that
is born of commercial pursuits and overeager self-help
gurus. I let such guesses pass me by while I wait upon
You and Your Word.

Hear me now, Lord. Do not let me wait in vain.
My eyes are watching and my ears are listening for the
Provider of hope and the final answers to all of life's
questions.

Tonight

*Surely then you will find delight in the Almighty and
will lift up your face to God. You will pray to him,
and he will hear you, and you will fulfill your vows.*

JOB 22:26-27

∾

The time will come when I will face the night with
hope. There will be anticipation as I plan to tell You
all about my troubles and my heartaches. Right now I
am still overcome with my trials. I know You are here,
carrying me through them, but I have been reluctant
to listen to what You have to tell me.

Tonight I will lift up my face to You and step into
Your presence wholly.

Breathing

Ah...

How can I, your servant, talk with you, my lord?
My strength is gone and I can hardly breathe.

DANIEL 10:17

～

I can hear my own breathing. It is rough with fatigue after my long day. As much as I love this time to talk with You, I barely have the energy to put together a few thoughts. Breathing in and out reminds me of how intricately I am formed. There are so many ways in which You keep my life in motion, even when I don't have the strength.

Resting in Your presence feels good. Do You mind if I stay quiet? The pace of my breathing reminds me of Your heartbeat.

My Time

You have made my days a mere handbreadth;
the span of my years is as nothing before you.
Each man's life is but a breath.

PSALM 39:5

✑

My focus is on my life. On what affects me. On
what I need. On who I know. On how I live. My personal experiences become my foundation. This is all
I know. But You who gave life to all of creation know
that my time to taste, feel, laugh, cry, and pray is limited. You want me to live more fully. Lord, give me the
capacity to love and feel and care with Your sensitivity
and understanding. May my vision extend beyond my
small world.

My life is but a breath. May I celebrate it.

In the Quiet

*They were glad when it grew calm, and he guided
them to their desired haven.*

PSALM 107:30

∽

Lead me to the stillness of this evening, God. Grant
my heart the peace it longs for. A busy day feels good,
but this time of quiet with You feels even better. Soothe
the rapid beating of my heart. Lengthen and deepen
my breaths so that I can rest and take in the gift of
renewal.

I'm not good at letting go of the day, Lord. But
tonight I give you my today and my tomorrow, and
allow myself to surrender to this moment of quiet in
Your arms.

How I Know

*But it is the spirit in a man, the breath of the
Almighty, that gives him understanding.*

JOB 32:8

∽

People ask me how I can believe in You when
there is such hardship and trouble in the world. I don't
always provide a great answer. But I do know that I
could not make sense of the world if I didn't have faith
in a loving Creator.

In my spirit is Your breath, Your wisdom, and Your
presence, Lord. You give me understanding that goes
beyond head knowledge. You anchor me in faith with
Your love and Your mercy. This is how I know to trust
the way of faith.

Preparation

Hearing the Voice

A voice of one calling in the desert, "Prepare the way for the Lord, make straight paths for him."

MATTHEW 3:3

When I was young, I didn't always heed the advice of my parents. There were times when I was outside playing that I would completely ignore their voices calling me in for bedtime. I have shrugged off wisdom and walked away from direction.

But when I heard the instruction to prepare my heart for You, I was ready to listen. My childhood resistances, my teen rebellion, my human need for self-reliance were no match for the hope of a faith and a future. Help me continue to prepare my heart and life for the lessons You have to teach me, Lord. I am eager to hear You.

Designer Faith

*In my Father's house are many rooms; if it were
not so, I would have told you. I am going there to
prepare a place for you.*

JOHN 14:2

∞

Fashions, trends, and marketing schemes can make
me rethink my own taste and can certainly redirect my
steps to head for the nearest store. In my spiritual life,
I have come to realize that as universal as Your love is,
Lord, You are very specific in how You speak to me and
how You lead me.

You didn't offer the world a rigid style of belief.
You could have removed my free will, my chance to
choose to worship and follow You. Instead, You give
me a designer faith. You crafted my life from the very
beginning. You molded my character and continue to
shape who I am becoming. And Your name is embla-
zoned on my heart, Lord.

What Comes Next

Therefore, prepare your minds for action; be self-controlled; set your hope fully on the grace to be given you when Jesus Christ is revealed.

1 PETER 1:13

∽

I get so caught up in asking questions about what will happen next that I forget to ask for Your help in the moment. All day today my mind was overflowing with scenarios of the future. I tried to make decisions based on hypothetical situations. It was exhausting.

Tonight, I am asking for Your strength, self-control, and hope to face my present. Only when I seek Your grace and vision for my life will I ever be prepared for whatever tomorrow brings.

I Just Need More

But God said to him, "You fool! This very night
your life will be demanded from you. Then who
will get what you have prepared for yourself?"

LUKE 12:20

∽

All I need to feel secure is a few more dollars in the
bank this month and a bigger house in the near future.
I also want a lot of money set aside for the future. If I
achieve a bit more status at work, then I will be set.

For too long I have thought these things. I looked
to money and possessions and four walls to prepare me
for my tomorrows and to keep me out of the cold. Yet
none of these will matter when I leave this earth. All
that worrying, plotting, and planning will have paved
the way to nowhere. Grant me security in You, Lord.

Restoration

For a Better Day

After two days he will revive us; on the third day
he will restore us, that we may live in his presence.

HOSEA 6:2

∽

I made it through today because I prayed often. My lips praised You for those promises still unfolding in my life. My tears were evidence of my need for You. I used to lament such times, but now I am understanding how Your faithfulness is evident when I hold on to You and wait patiently for a better day.

That day of revival might be tomorrow, it might be next week, it could even come after months of waiting, but I am certain it will arrive. This hope carries me, Lord.

In Your Power

*How I long for your precepts! Preserve my life in
your righteousness.*

PSALM 119:40

✑

The day fades and so does the façade I have been
wearing all day. I want to come clean and strip away all
pretense and ego. I cannot do it on my own. I muddle
things up, and I seem to revisit the same life lessons
over and over.

Lord, I'm sorry that I lean on my own understanding so often. Save me from my stubbornness. Halt
my efforts to be my own healer and teacher, and preserve my life in your righteous knowledge and peace.

Praise

Fill Me, Lead Me

I will praise the LORD, who counsels me; even at
night my heart instructs me.

PSALM 16:7

✎

I am not afraid of the darkness that falls tonight.
All day I have been waiting for it, looking forward to
a special time to seek Your instruction. My days are
filled with many questions and decisions, so at night
my heart hungers for Your counsel.

Guide me, Lord. You are holy and mighty. Even
while I sleep, You tell my heart about the secrets of the
universe and about the wonders of Your leading.

Every Hour

*I will extol the LORD at all times; his praise will
always be on my lips.*

PSALM 34:1

❧

Like the church hymn says, I profess that I need
Thee every hour, Lord. Even when I do not acknowl-
edge that fact every moment of my day, it is true. I rely
on Your strength and insight and compassion. May my
actions and my words and my thoughts reflect Your
goodness at all times.

May praise fall from my lips and rise to be heard in
the heavens, Lord. And may my gratitude for the new
life You offer be expressed in who I am so that others
will see a reflection of You, my merciful God.

Who Has Loved Me

Praise be to God, who has not rejected my prayer or withheld his love from me!

PSALM 66:20

∽

I have felt left alone. Forgotten. Overlooked. Unheard. I have raised my voice and my fist to the air, Lord. You remember. Caught up in my sorrow and my questions, I doubted Your love. But You never left my side. You have never thrown up Your hands and said, "Forget it. This person is off My list."

When I recall the times I was not praying because it hurt too much, I know that my heart was lifting up cries for love and help on my behalf. And You heard me... every time. Praise be to God, for You are faithful.

Day or Night

*Then will I ever sing praise to your name and fulfill
my vows day after day.*

PSALM 61:8

❧

No matter the time of day, I will sing praises to Your
name, God. I will become more aware of how I live out
my faith and how I extend the grace You have extended
to me. I will honor You with acts of kindness, courage,
and compassion.

Each day is a new chance to display Your goodness
through my words and actions. Was today a pleasing
offering to You, Lord? Did I step into and through all
that You had for me? As I lie down to sleep, my spirit
continues to sing praises because it is thankful for Your
love, no matter the hour.

All That I Have

*May my prayer be set before you like incense;
may the lifting up of my hands be like the evening sacrifice.*

PSALM 141:2

∽

It isn't much, this offering of my life, but it is
all that I have to give. It isn't much, this day I have
lived, but it is all that I know right now. My praise
might not sound like the salutation of angels, but
it is all my lips can form.

My heart is often empty, but it is ready to be
filled by Your love. My future is uncertain, but it is
Yours to shape. My prayer tonight is much like it
is every night, but it is born of my spirit of gratitude. May You receive these humble offerings with
pleasure and grace. Amen.

The One-Minute Prayers™ series